ALL YOU WA

Walking

VIJAYA KUMAR

New Dawn

NEW DAWN
a division of Sterling Publishers (P) Ltd.
A-59, Okhla Industrial Area, Phase-II, New Delhi-110020.
Tel: 26387070, 26386209; Fax: 91-11-26383788
E-mail: info@sterlingpublishers.com
www.sterlingpublishers.com

All You Wanted to Know about Walking
© 2002, Sterling Publishers Private Limited
ISBN 81 207 2437 2
Reprint 2005

Published by Sterling Publishers Pvt. Ltd., New Delhi-110020.
Lasertypeset by Vikas Compographics New Delhi-110020.
Printed at Sai Early Learners (P) Ltd., New Delhi-110020.

Contents

Contents

Introduction

Walking is the safest and most convenient activity for weight control, ailment-free health, and all-round physical fitness. But walking is much more than these — it is about growth, success, determination, dedication, about an 'I can' and an 'I will' attitude, and about the pleasures of walking.

This book includes programmes for diet-conscious people, beginners, the aged, and for a health-conscious lifestyle.

In just about two months of this programme, you can expect firmer muscles, stronger bones, fewer inches around the waist, thighs and buttocks, and fewer tensions, leading to a healthier and more active life.

Did you know that walking uses large portions of muscle groups in your legs and arms in a steady, rhythmic pattern? No wonder it is recommended for not just fitness but for total health too. It is the cornerstone of a total approach to personal fitness. Walking is one exercise that offers multiple advantages at a minimum cost and with least effort.

Walk Slim

Walking uses the muscles of the legs and hips, and the arm swing gives the shoulders and arms a workout. Here is some useful information if you have decided on a walking programme.

- In the first week of your programme, walk 10 minutes every day, without stopping.
- In the second week, increase the duration to 15 minutes, making the walk a little brisker.
- Gradually, step up the duration to at least an hour, if not longer. By the end of the month it is good if you are doing two hours at a stretch.

- It is always better to start walking exercises before going on a diet, since walking will keep you motivated to achieve your goal.
- The pace at which you walk should be suited to your physical conditions.
- You can gradually step up your pace to a brisk aerobic walk that will make you feel good.
- Aerobic walking is brisk, rhythmic movements that gets you into a comfortable stride and helps you to burn off around 200 calories every 30 minutes, as your metabolic rate increases.
- To begin with, check your height and weight against the chart given on pages 10 and 11).

- For a woman, the weight should be nearer the lower figure in the weight range, and for a man, depending on his build, it should be towards the higher figure.
- Warm-up exercises should be done once you start walking for an hour.
- The idea behind these warm-ups is to help you to improve performance and prevent injury to any part of the body.
- The simple exercises help to raise the pulse rate and to have better blood and fluid circulation to the muscles, joints, ligaments, etc.
- Your hamstrings, calves, Achilles tendons and quadriceps are exercised for warmth and relaxation, and for a good walking rhythm.

Ideal Height/Weight Chart

Height			Weight	
ft	in	cm	lbs	kg
Women over 25 years				
4	10	147.3	96 – 107	43.5 – 48.5
4	12	149.9	98 – 110	44.5 – 49.9
5	0	152.4	101 – 113	45.8 – 51.3
5	1	154.9	104 – 116	47.2 – 52.6
5	2	157.5	107 – 119	48.5 – 54.0
5	3	160.0	110 – 122	49.5 – 55.3
5	4	162.6	113 – 126	51.3 – 57.2
5	5	165.1	116 – 130	52.6 – 59.0
5	6	167.6	120 – 135	54.4 – 61.2
5	7	170.2	124 – 139	56.2 – 63.0
5	8	172.7	128 – 143	58.1 – 64.9
5	9	175.3	132 – 147	59.9 – 66.7
5	10	177.8	136 – 151	61.7 – 68.5
5	11	180.3	140 – 155	63.5 – 70.3
6	0	182.9	144 – 159	65.3 – 72.0

Ideal Height/Weight Chart

Height			Weight	
ft	in	cm	lbs	kg
Men over 25 years				
5	2	157.5	118 – 129	53.5 – 58.5
5	3	160.0	121 – 133	54.9 – 60.3
5	4	162.6	124 – 136	56.2 – 61.7
5	5	165.1	127 – 139	57.6 – 63.0
5	6	167.6	130 – 143	59.0 – 64.9
5	7	170.2	134 – 147	60.8 – 66.7
5	8	172.7	138 – 152	62.6 – 68.9
5	9	175.3	142 – 156	64.4 – 70.8
5	10	177.8	146 – 160	66.2 – 72.6
5	11	180.3	150 – 165	68.0 – 74.8
6	0	182.9	154 – 170	69.9 – 77.1
6	1	185.4	158 – 175	71.7 – 79.4
6	2	188.0	162 – 180	73.5 – 81.6

Warm-up exercises
Shoulder circles

- Stand straight, hands by the side, feet a foot apart (relaxes neck, shoulders, back).

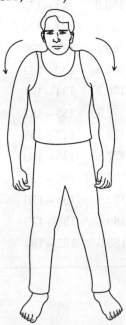

- Lift shoulders, rotate back, down and forward in a circular motion 10 times.

Arms raise

- Stand erect, feet a foot apart, hands by the side.

- Raise both arms up from the sides to the top, and inhale simultaneously.
- Lower arms to the sides as you exhale. Repeat 9 times (relaxes shoulders and chest).

Knee lifts

- March on the spot 16 times.
- Lift legs at least six inches from the floor.
- Swing hands, with arms bent slightly at the elbows (warms up calves, Achilles tendons and quadriceps).

Thigh stretch

- Stand on left leg with knee slightly bent, supporting yourself with the back of a chair.

15

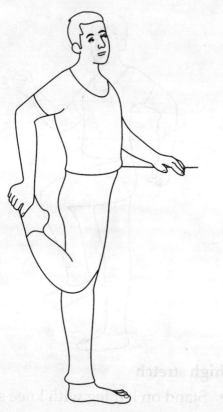

- Bend right foot backwards, and grip the foot with the right hand, easing the toes towards the right buttock.

- Hold for 15 seconds.
- Repeat with the other leg.
- Repeat both the leg exercises four times (gently stretches the quadriceps).

Hamstring stretch

- Placing hands on the left thigh, bend the left leg.
- Straighten out the right leg in front of you, pointing toes, knees in line.
- Lean forward slightly, tucking in stomach.
- Hold for 15 seconds.
- Repeat with the other leg.

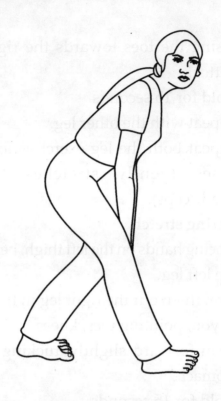

- Do this set four more times (eases thigh muscles).

18

Calf raise

- Using a wall or chair for support, stand erect, shoulders back and relaxed, stomach pulled in.

- Raise body on the balls of the feet and hold for a couple of seconds.
- Lower heels to the floor.
- Repeat four times (warms up calf muscles and Achilles tendons).

Calf stretch
- Stand one and a half feet away from a wall.
- Place right foot six inches from the wall, in line with the left foot.
- Gradually bend forward, and place both palms on the wall, feet remaining flat on the floor.
- Hold for 15 seconds.
- Repeat with the other foot.

- Do this set four more times (stretches out the calf and Achilles tendons).

Ankle rotation

- Holding on to some support, raise one foot slightly from the floor.

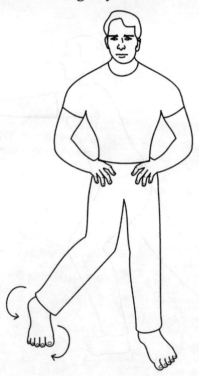

- Rotate it first in one direction five times, then in the opposite direction five times.
- Repeat with the other foot.

Cooling Down

- When you stop exercising, you need to cool down gradually. Lying down immediately to rest may not always be advisable as that can bring trouble.
- Either cool down by walking slowly for a few minutes, or sit down on the ground with your feet out so that the blood does not have to flow vertically uphill from the legs to return to the heart.

- Do not take a shower immediately after your workout.

Stretching the lower back

- From the standing position, slowly bend forward at the waist and hang down towards your toes.

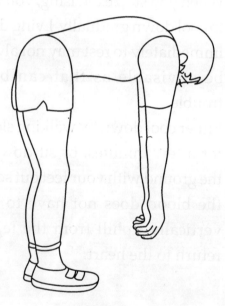

- Keep the legs straight, balancing evenly on the feet, arms hanging loosely.
- Remain stretched for 30 seconds.
- Slowly return to standing position.

Stretching the calf muscles

- Place both hands on one knee, and bring the other leg back, so that one foot is about 2 feet behind the other.
- The heel of the back foot should be flat on the ground.
- The part of the front leg below the knee should be vertical.
- You may press against the forward knee to help the stretching.
- Remain stretched for 30 seconds.

- Slowly return to original position by bringing the hips back.
- Repeat this stretch for the other calf.

Stretching the upper back and neck

- Grasp both your elbows.
- Bend your head and shoulder forward with your chin on your chest.

26

- Remain stretched for 30 seconds.
- Release slowly.

Stretch for the groin

- Place one foot behind the other, one and a half feet apart.

- Bend the left leg at the knee, and stretch the right foot straight back, toes touching the ground, and hands on the ground for support.
- Remain stretched for 30 seconds, then release slowly.
- Repeat for the other side.

28

Perfect posture

- A good posture helps to tone your body, improve the blood circulation, and prevent injuries.
- A good posture helps the body in maintaining a good rhythm and balance.
- Do not slouch, but walk tall, with back straight and shoulders relaxed.
- Take long strides that you are comfortable with, letting your arms swing naturally, shoulders relaxed.
- Breathe naturally, inhaling and exhaling rhythmically through the nose.

Ideal heart rate

- A brisk aerobic walk between three and a half to four miles per hour will burn calories more quickly and more efficiently.

- If you walk intensely, your heart beat can be stepped up between 60 per cent and 80 per cent of its maximum rate.

- To find out your ideal pulse rate or target heart rate, subtract your age from 220 — the maximum heart rate, *e.g.* if you are 50 years old, then your target heart rate would be 220-50=170.

- Now calculate 60 per cent and 80 per cent of your maximum heart rate.

$$\frac{170 \times 60}{100} = 102 \qquad \frac{170 \times 80}{100} = 136$$

Your target heart rate should be between 102 and 136 beats per minute, according to this example.

- If your target heart rate is below the lower end of the range, increase your walking speed, and if it is above the higher end of the range, slow down.

When to Walk

- Walking should be done whenever you find the time convenient.
- Early morning hours are best for walking, for there are less distractions and less traffic.
- Taking a morning walk is also a good weight management strategy for those who are tempted to snack in the morning.
- For people working outside the home, lunchtime is the ideal time, when you walk or climb several flights of stairs, after a light meal.
- Brisk walking in the noontime helps you to ward off an afternoon nap,

and also increase your productivity over the next few hours.

- A 15-minute break can be utilised for brisk walking, which is quite refreshing.
- Some like to take an evening walk, before or after dinner.
- Walking before dinner reduces hunger pangs that one feels in the early evening hours, and thus helps control the urge to eat before dinner.
- Some people prefer to walk after dinner to alleviate the tight, full feeling that sometimes makes you feel uncomfortable and sleepy.
- After-dinner walking also helps in burning fat by elevating the basal metabolism in the body, but wait for

an hour after eating before you commence your walk.

- Be consistent in your walking schedule, incorporating walking on a regular basis into your daily routine.
- Always plan your day around your walking and not your walking around your day.

Where to Walk

- Choose where you would like to walk — indoors or outdoors.
- Though you may walk indoors on some days (especially on a rainy day), and outdoors on other days, you will probably enjoy both.
- Use your imagination and creativity to find areas for walking that are best for you.
- Make your walking exercise enjoyable so that it never becomes a tedious chore to be done.
- Any indoor area that is spacious enough for continuous walking, and that will not bore you, is adequate.

- Two good indoor walking places are hotels and shopping malls, where you can climb each flight of stairs and walk around the hall of each floor.
- Another good place is a university area which is normally a vast expanse of space.
- The large halls of schools are excellent for sustained walking.
- Most people prefer to walk indoors as it helps in consistency, is convenient, adds variety to your daily walk, and is safe.
- Public parks are ideal for a relaxing stroll, and also for brisk walking in the early hours of the morning when strollers are few.

- A stadium is another area which provides a good place for a few laps.
- Walking with nature in any season gives us the opportunity to capture the best of both worlds: pure enjoyment and the return to our roots.
- A walk in the woods would be exhilarating. The peace and serenity of the woods offers a calming and soothing effect that cannot be found anywhere else.
- Leave all your valuables at home, including your purse.
- If possible, walk on a main thoroughfare.
- You may carry an umbrella or a walking stick.

- Do not walk alone at night.
- Do not wear provocative clothes, or stop and talk to strangers.
- Carry small change for an emergency telephone call.
- Let your family or a friend know your walking route, and when you are expected to return.
- Carry a piece of identification.
- If time permits, walk to work.
- When you take your car, park your car further away than your normal parking slot, and walk the extra distance to your workplace.
- Whenever you get an opportunity, use the stairs instead of a lift.

Workplan

- Lao Tse said, "The journey of a thousand miles begins with just one step." So, do not just sit there — but start walking.
- Once you have made a resolution to walk every day, all you then need is motivation and a plan to develop fitness and robust health.
- Never get into vigorous fitness walking without gradually building up to it.
- With aging, muscle fibre declines gradually, but walking will help you regain some of that lost muscle strength.

- Walking is the best and cheapest form of exercise, the only essential item being a pair of comfortable walking shoes.
- Start walking slowly and gradually and as you feel comfortable with the pace, increase your pace.
- Check your weight every week, and as you see yourself shedding excess weight gradually, your motivation to keep going becomes stronger.
- Walking with others helps you in warding off any form of boredom.
- Maintain a record of your progress — your speed, time, distance covered, target heart rate and weight.

40

- If your initial enthusiasm wanes, do not give up, but continue walking, setting yourself achievable goals.
- Do not forget your warm-ups and cool-downs before and after walking.
- Treat your body with gentleness and care.
- To make your walking a regular habit, you can start walking close to your home, so that you do not come up with excuses, like the road is too steep, or the park is too far, etc.
- Always walk to suit your physical condition and listen to the dictates of your body — do not push yourself beyond your capacity.

Walking Aids

- It is very important to begin developing a mindset that will keep you a serious and committed walker forever.
- One way to prepare yourself is with a stack of various aids in walking.
- Aids, referring to the usefulness or necessity in achieving an end, can be in the form of equipment and instruments that provide comfort and ease of mobility—like shoes and clothes.
- They can also be in the form of strategies and techniques which are

used to help assist in achieving long-term goals.

- A clear advantage that walkers have over joggers and other sportspeople is simplicity in attire.
- In general, any shoe that is comfortable and feels good can be used for walking.
- Since walking is going to be your lifetime routine, you need shoes that will add pleasure, maximise comfort, and minimise the possibility of injury.
- Your walking shoes should fit snugly, like a glove, at the heel and the instep, and should conform to the natural outline of your foot.

- Your toes should have enough space in front to lift, wiggle and spread without difficulty.
- The heels of the shoes should be broad enough with double or triple layers, to give adequate support to absorb the impact of the weight of your body.
- Avoid using high-heeled shoes for long walks.
- The inner padding in the soles and heels should be soft and spongy to absorb the impact of walking, but rough enough for the socks to have a grip on them.
- In general, shoes should be pliable, durable and 'breathable' to allow proper aeration and ventilation.

44

- The best time for purchasing shoes is in the afternoon or early evening when your feet swell during the day.
- When you are buying shoes, go in for their functionability rather than the look. If they look good, it is a bonus.
- Remember that one foot is always slightly larger than the other, so try the shoe on the larger foot first.
- It is usually recommended that you break your new shoes in gradually by wearing them around the house.
- Good leather shoes will breathe and allow fresh air to circulate and cool your feet, and simultaneously allow perspiration to evaporate.
- The socks that you wear should be either cotton or woollen and should

fit snugly. It should provide a good fit with room enough for flexing your toes.

- Your attire for walking should be comfortable, practical, light and loose.
- In the cold season, step out comfortably attired and well protected from coldness.
- In bright and hot weather, wear light-coloured clothes, and protect your head with a cap or hat.
- If you feel comfortable with a walking stick, do take it with you — it could also be a good defensive weapon!
- A pedometer, a small precision instrument that records the number

of miles walked, can be hooked to your belt, trousers or skirt.

- If you are not sure how far you have travelled, a pedometer then becomes invaluable.
- Keep a walking chart in a conspicuous place in your house, showing you graphically the number of miles you have walked over several days or weeks.
- The chart is also useful in maintaining or increasing your motivation to achieve a long-range walking goal.

Family Fitness

- Children are, by and large, very active, but they too can be prone to obesity, hypertension and high blood cholesterol if they are inactive and lead a sedentary life, or have poor nutrition.

- Television, modern transport system, video games, etc., restrict a child's activities, leading to poor health.

- If the school is not too far, a child should practise walking to school, and back home.

- Parents should encourage their children to walk more often, and they too can join them in their walk, adding more spice and zest to this simple exercise.

- If your child gasps for breath after climbing a flight or two of stairs, then he is not fit.
- Doctors recommend that walking is better than running for children, because it prevents injuries to legs.
- Children who walk regularly enhance their flexibility, stamina and strength.
- Walking helps a child to develop good posture.
- It promotes strong bone growth, thus preventing the chance of osteoporosis later in life.

- Walking helps a child to be physically and mentally more aware and alert.
- A child who walks regularly every day develops firm muscles, and is free of back pain.
- When all the members of a family set out for a walk together, the exercise becomes enjoyable and is a great escape from television, computer, video games, etc.
- Family walks provide a good time and occasion for togetherness, for this is one exercise in which everyone can participate.
- Walking is also the only exercise in which everyone sets out on an equal footing.

- It not only builds up a good strong body packed with health and stamina but also accounts for a strong and healthy family bond.
- Since boredom can become an excuse for discontinuing your walks together, you must ensure that walking is full of fun.
- You can change your walking route after a week or so, as a change of scenery will keep the enthusiasm alive.
- Occasionally, or on holidays, indulge in nature walk, which will enhance children's awareness and appreciation of the surroundings and the environment.

- A zoo, playground, museum or stadium can also be considered for walking.
- Make sure that kids at first walk regularly than walk too fast or too far.
- Always walk on or near the pavement.
- Before crossing a street, look both ways twice before stepping out on to the road.
- A good safety precaution is to walk facing the oncoming traffic, so that you can see what is approaching.
- Women of any age can walk and gain significant benefits.
- Walking is the best exercise during pregnancy and labour.

Fitness for the Aged

- Walking is the most effective and inexpensive form of exercise for the aged, and the only one that one can follow all the years of one's life.
- Walking is the most beneficial exercise for the elderly, as it is safe, simple and easy to do.
- For older men and women alike, walking helps to maintain a long and healthy life.
- Walking can decrease the probability of fractures, that older people are increasingly susceptible to, by improving agility and balance.

- If one does fracture a bone, recovery is also hastened by the increase in resiliency as a result of walking.
- Walking is one of the exercises frequently recommended to women for the treatment and prevention of osteoporosis, which usually sets in after the age of 50.
- Elderly people can therefore receive tremendous physical benefits and become less susceptible to injuries by walking more.
- If you have guests staying with you, you could invite them too for a walk — the pleasant activity that endures through the ages.
- Walk at a pace that you are comfortable with, and wear your most comfortable shoes.

- Focus on enjoyment, not speed.
- Do not walk too far, for you may find it very tiring.
- Avoid stopping and talking, just nod and smile, and keep moving.
- Do not put walking today for tomorrow.
- Walk steadily and with a purpose.
- Just remember, walking slows down the aging process, and could make you look younger, fitter and more energetic.
- Walking also helps to alleviate back pain, arthritis, cholesterol level, osteoporosis, varicose veins and diabetes.
- You can cut your rate of physical decline by walking regularly.

- Walking is beneficial to the respiratory system. You can breathe easily without having a feeling of constriction.

- You find your muscle endurance improving with sustained walking.

- Walking raises the good cholesterol HDL — High Density Lipoproteins and guards against heart ailments.

- It is important, to have a regular check-up with your doctor.

- If you are obese, start your walk at a slow pace, gradually increasing the speed till you are walking comfortably at a brisk rate.

- You will soon find yourself motivated by shedding off all unwanted fat.

The Fitness Walker's Diet

- The key to both healthy eating and weight loss is to revamp your eating habits — eating more complex carbohydrates, fruits and vegetables, and avoiding fat, sugar and excess salt.

- Most people put on all the weight that they had so laboriously shed off simply because their diet was not combined with exercises.

- Dieting may give you the feeling that you have lost weight, when in fact, all that you have lost is tissues and muscles, and not fat.

- Dieting, unaccompanied by any form of exercise, leads to a slowdown in the basal metabolism rate, resulting in conservation of fat in the body.
- Slimming foods offering miracle weight loss in quick time, without the hassles of exercising, are just fads, and you must be careful not to fall into such traps.
- In order to lose weight, be fit and maintain good health, it is essential to diet and exercise.
- The key to successful dieting and exercise is moderation.
- Remember that aerobic walking activates your metabolism and burns fat.

- The central focus of a walker's diet is on eating fat sparingly.
- Carbohydrates (one gram contains four calories) are necessary to digest, absorb and store calories internally.
- It is the nature of our body to burn carbohydrates and store fat.
- Walking briskly will burn stored fat after the first 20 minutes.
- If you walk 30 minutes at a brisk pace, you will burn 200 calories.
- By walking regularly your metabolism increases, which with the help of oxygen, burns off fuel (food), converting it into heat and energy.
- Research shows that walking first thing in the morning, when glycogen reserves are very low,

helps you to lose weight quicker, since energy is produced by using the stored body fat.

- To maintain your weight, a well-balanced diet is essential.
- Complex carbohydrates, like rice, bread, potatoes, cereals, etc., and fruits and vegetables are the key to health and vitality, weight control, and also to ward off cancer and heart diseases.
- The Food Guide Pyramid (given on the next page) released by the US Department of Agriculture shows the main foods at a glance—eat more of the foods at the base of the pyramid, and less of the foods at the top.

Food Guide Pyramid

Fats, oils
Use sparingly

Added sugar, sweets,
aerated drinks
Use infrequently

Milk, yoghurt
and cheese
*2-3 servings
daily*

Meat, poultry,
fish, dry beans,
eggs and nuts
*2-3 servings
daily*

Vegetables
*3-5 servings
daily*

Fruits
*2-4 servings
daily*

Bread, cereal, rice

6-11 servings daily

- Do not consider what is good or bad, just which food to increase or decrease according to the pyramid.
- Use dairy products less as they are all high in fat.
- You can use skimmed milk instead of full-fat milk.
- Substitute low-fat margarine for butter and lard.
- Natural yoghurt is a good substitute for cream, or else use low-fat cream.
- Lemon and lime juice are preferable to salad dressing or mayonnaise.
- Instead of rich desserts, eat fresh fruits.
- Avoid eating biscuits, cakes and crisps.

- Wholemeal bread or wheat bread (brown bread) makes a satisfying addition to a meal.
- Porridge at breakfast is a good source of energy, and is very satisfying.
- Tomatoes, mushrooms or baked beans can be eaten with wholemeal toast for breakfast.
- Fruits are a good source of fibre that the body needs and which gives you the feeling of fullness of a meal.
- Fish is a rich source of vitamins and minerals.
- If you eat eggs, cook them using very little fat — poached or boiled is preferred.
- You can also scramble an egg or prepare an omelette in a non-stick

pan, adding tomatoes, carrots, onions and mushrooms to it.

- Fruit or vegetable juice provides immediate energy.
- Have a glass of fresh juice the first thing in the morning—it gives instant vitality and a feeling of well-being.
- Experts state that 35 per cent of all cancers are related to diet, and vitamin C, vitamin E and beta-carotene eliminate free radicals, thus protecting against cancer and heart diseases.
- Vitamins A, C and E are found in the following:

Beta-carotene (a form of vitamin A): Dark leafy green vegetables, yellow and orange fruits and vegetables (spinach, peas, asparagus, broccoli, carrots, tomatoes, pumpkin, sweet potatoes, tomatoes, apricots, melons, cherries, peaches, mangoes, etc.).

Vitamin C: Citrus fruits, raw cabbage, green leafy vegetables, capsicum, tomatoes, potatoes, parsnips, oranges, strawberries, blackcurrants, kiwi fruit, etc.

Vitamin E: Nuts, soyabeans, wholegrains, seeds, green leafy vegetables, sunflower oil, fish liver oil, etc.

- Follow a diet which is based on low-fat, high-fibre foods.

Recipes for Staying Fit and Trim

The following recipes are for two persons. Salt is optional.

Garden Salad

> 2 carrots, grated
>
> 1 stick celery, thinly cut
>
> 1 cucumber, cut into wedges
>
> 1 large pear (or seasonal fruit like apple), diced
>
> juice of 1 lemon
>
> 2 tomatoes, cut into wedges
>
> freshly ground black pepper and salt to taste

Arrange the grated carrot in a tray. Place the celery, cucumber, tomato and pear over the carrot. Add the lemon juice. Sprinkle some salt and add the freshly ground pepper.

Juscan Salad

1 tin tuna in brine (drained)

150 gms cooked beans (preferably lobiyan or white beans)

1 small onion, chopped

1 tsp olive oil

½ tsp vinegar or red wine

1 tsp parsley, chopped

½ tsp freshly ground black pepper

lemon wedges

salt to taste (optional)

Combine the tuna, beans and half of the chopped onion. Arrange on a plate. Mix together in a bowl, the olive oil, vinegar and parsley, and pour over the salad. Arrange the remaining chopped onion on it, and add the ground pepper. Garnish with the lemon wedges.

Italian Salad

a few salad leaves
4 thin slices of salami, cut into pieces
2 small cucumber pieces, chopped small
2 spring onions, chopped
1 large tomato, cut into wedges
a few black olives
a few fresh basil (tulsi) leaves
½ a lemon
freshly ground black pepper to taste

Arrange the salad leaves on a plate. Place the salami, cucumber, spring onion and tomato over the leaves. Squeeze the lemon over the salad,

and sprinkle the pepper. Garnish
with olives and basil leaves.

Mediterranean Salad

1 big tomato, sliced
75 gms cheese, cubed
a few fresh basil leaves, chopped
juice of ½ a lemon
freshly ground black pepper to taste

Arrange the tomato slices on a plate.
Place the cheese cubes on them.
Spread the chopped basil leaves
over them. Squeeze the lemon over
the salad, and sprinkle some pepper.

Spanish Salad

a few lettuce leaves
1 large tomato, thinly sliced
1 small capsicum, cut into rings
1 small onion, thinly sliced

1 small tin tuna in brine (drained and
   flaked)
6 asparagus spears, cooked
2 hard-boiled eggs, quartered
1 tsp lemon juice
freshly ground black pepper to taste
Arrange the lettuce leaves on a
plate, and place the tomato,
capsicum and onion over them.
Arrange the asparagus spears, egg
quarters and tuna as the third layer.
Pour the lemon juice over it, and
sprinkle some black pepper.

Russian Salad

75 gms beetroot, grated and cooked
75 gms potatoes, cut and cooked
75 gms carrots, cut and cooked
2 tsps mayonnaise

1 tsp lemon juice

1 tsp tomato sauce

freshly ground black pepper to taste

Mix together the mayonnaise, lemon juice and sauce. Add the potatoes and carrots to this mixture. Stir gently so that all the pieces are evenly coated with the mixture. Arrange the grated beetroot on a plate. Spread the salad mixture over the beetroot. Add the lemon juice, and then the pepper over the salad.

Spring Salad

a few lettuce leaves, shredded

100 gms sweetcorn

2 hard-boiled eggs, quartered

2 tsps pumpkin seeds

2 tsps mayonnaise

freshly ground black pepper to taste

Arrange the lettuce on a plate. Mix together the sweetcorn, pumpkin seeds and mayonnaise, and add to the leaves. Arrange the egg quarters on the salad, sprinkle them with the pepper.

Apple and Carrot Salad

2 carrots, finely grated

3 apples, finely grated with skin

a handful of chopped coriander leaves

1 chilli, chopped

juice of 1 lemon

1 small cucumber, grated with skin

freshly ground black pepper and salt to taste

Arrange the apple, carrot and cucumber gratings on a plate. Pour the lemon juice over them. Sprinkle the pepper and salt, and add the chopped chillies. Garnish with the chopped coriander leaves.

Pineapple - Beetroot Salad

1 small beetroot, peeled and grated
1 small pineapple, cut into small pieces
juice of 1 lemon
a bunch of chopped coriander leaves
freshly ground black pepper and salt to
    taste

Arrange the beetroot gratings on a plate. Layer these with the pineapple pieces. Pour the lemon juice over the salad. Add salt and pepper, and garnish with the coriander leaves.

Pear with Orange

1 small pear, cubed
1 large orange, peeled and deseeded
2 tsps sesame seeds, toasted
juice of ½ a lemon
a few salad leaves

Arrange the salad leaves and place the orange segments over them decoratively. Layer these with the pear cubes. Spoon the lemon juice over these. Garnish with the toasted sesame seeds.

Cabbage and Apple Mayonnaise

1 small cabbage, finely shredded
2 apples, diced with skin
2 tsps sesame seeds
2 tsps mayonnaise
2 tsps yoghurt (from skimmed milk)

1 tsp fresh mint, chopped

freshly ground black pepper to taste

Combine the mayonnaise, yoghurt and mint. Add the cabbage and apple pieces and stir well. Arrange on a plate, and sprinkle the sesame seeds and pepper powder over the salad.

Prawns - Grapes with Egg Mayonnaise

2 hard-boiled eggs, halved

75 gms cooked prawns

75 gms seedless grapes

2 tsps mayonnaise

2 tsps yoghurt (from skimmed milk)

2 lemon wedges

freshly ground black pepper to taste

Arrange the eggs on a tray. Mix together the prawns, grapes, mayonnaise and yoghurt, and spread over the eggs. Garnish with pepper and the lemon wedges.

Savoury Rice Flakes

1 cup rice flakes (chiwda)
1 cup yoghurt (from skimmed milk)
1 green chilli, chopped
chopped coriander leaves for garnishing
1 tbsp grated coconut
salt to taste

Soak the rice flakes in the yoghurt, mixed with 2 tbsps of water. Add salt and the other ingredients, and stir well. Garnish with the coriander leaves.

Macaroni Salad

60 gms macaroni, cooked and cooled
1 bunch celery, diced

115 gms cabbage, shredded
55 gms capsicum, chopped
1 spring onion, chopped
1 lemon, cut into wedges
1 bunch lettuce
1 cup mayonnaise
4 small red radish, sliced

Mix the celery, cabbage, capsicum and spring onion with the macaroni. Add the mayonnaise. Arrange the lettuce leaves around the sides of salad bowl. Put in the macaroni mixture. Garnish with the red radish slices and lemon wedges.

Cheese and Peas Salad

50 gms cottage cheese, cubed
½ cup peas, boiled
1 large onion, chopped

1 small capsicum, chopped

2 tbsps mayonnaise

1 tsp cream

freshly ground black pepper and salt to
   taste

Mix together the cheese, capsicum, peas and onion. Add the mayonnaise, pepper and salt and stir lightly. Dot with the cream on top.

Sprouts Salad

1 cup mixed sprouts, cooked with salt

1 raw mango, grated

¼ cup grated cheese

lemon juice

1 tsp honey

freshly ground black pepper

mint leaves for garnishing

Mix the sprouts with all the other ingredients except the last two. Sprinkle the pepper over the salad and garnish with the mint leaves.

Egg-Spinach Salad

220 gms spinach, chopped

1 tsp tomato sauce

1 tsp chilli sauce

2 eggs, poached

freshly ground black pepper and salt to taste

Boil the spinach with very little water. Add the chilli, tomato sauces and salt, and mix well. Arrange on a plate, with the egg on top. Sprinkle the pepper, and serve with toast.

Tomato Pachadi

2 tomatoes, chopped
1 small cucumber, chopped
2 tbsps coconut gratings
2 green chillies
coriander leaves, chopped
½ tsp mustard seeds
2 cups yoghurt
1 tsp oil
salt to taste

Grind the coconut and chillies and mix with the yoghurt. Add this to the rest of the ingredients, and garnish with the coriander leaves.

Gingered Beans

125 gms beans, cut into 1" pieces
2 tsps fresh ginger juice

2 tsps oil
½ tsp mustard
½ tsp cumin seeds
salt to taste

Boil the beans with salt. Heat oil and fry the seasonings in a pan. Stir in the beans. Pour the ginger juice over it and cook on a high flame for a minute, stirring the mixture well. Garnish with the coriander leaves.

Yam Delight

125 gms yam, cubed
1 cup curd
½ tsp gram flour
a pinch of turmeric powder and asafoetida
2 green chillies
2 tsps freshly ground coconut

a small piece of ginger
coriander leaves
1 tsp ghee
½ tsp mustard seeds
salt

Mix the curd, gram flour, turmeric powder, salt and asafoetida. Grind together the coconut, ginger and chillies. Add to the curd mixture. Mix the yam in it. Pressure cook the mixture and cool. Fry the seasoning in ghee and pour this over the yam. Serve hot.

Curdy Potatoes

3 potatoes, cubed
1 cup curd, beaten
1 tsp cumin seeds
1 tsp chopped coriander leaves

½ tsp chilli powder

2 green chillies, chopped

2 tbsps oil

salt to taste

In hot oil, splutter the cumin seeds. Add the potatoes, green chillies and chilli and turmeric powder. Add salt and one cup water, and cook till done. Add the curd and cook till the potatoes are soft. Garnish with the coriander leaves.

Baked Tomatoes with Mushrooms

2 large ripe tomatoes

200 gms mushrooms, finely chopped

1 onion, finely chopped

1 egg, beaten

1 tsp lemon juice

coriander leaves, chopped

freshly ground pepper and
salt to taste
1 tsp oil

Remove the top from the tomatoes, scoop out the pulp, sprinkle a little salt inside the tomatoes, and place them upside down for an hour. In one tsp oil fry the onions and mushrooms lightly. Stir in the lemon juice and salt. Cook till the water has evaporated. Cool, then add the yolk and mix well. Fill this in the tomatoes and bake. Remove and garnish with the coriander leaves.

Cheese and Egg on Toast

4 eggs, separated
30 gms cheese, grated
freshly ground pepper to taste

2 tsps oil

salt to taste

Beat the egg whites stiff with salt. Heat the oil and add the egg whites and pepper. Divide the egg whites into four portions, and make a hollow in the centre of each. Place in yolk in each, and sprinkle cheese on top. Place under a grill, and cook on a slow fire till the cheese has melted. Place each portion on a toast and serve immediately.

Baked Vegetable Omelette

2 eggs

½ cup diced vegetables (carrots, beans, capsicum, tomatoes, peas, etc.)

1 green chilli, chopped

coriander leaves, chopped

1 *tbsp chopped onion*
2 *tsps grated cheese*
1 *tsp oil*
freshly ground black pepper and
salt to taste

Boil the vegetables, except the tomatoes. Fry the onions lightly. Add the vegetables, chilli, coriander leaves, salt and pepper. Remove from fire after a minute of sauteing. Add the tomatoes. Beat the eggs till stiff. Grease a flat ovenproof dish and pour the eggs into it. Lightly strew the vegetables over them. Bake till almost set. Sprinkle the cheese over the mixture and bake for another 10 minutes. Cut into slices and serve with toast.

Baked Potato Sandwiches

4 potatoes, boiled and grated

4 slices bread, soaked and squeezed dry

4 green chillies, chopped

1 tsp chopped coriander leaves

juice of 1 lemon

½ tsp red chilli powder

1 bunch mint leaves

salt to taste

Mix the potato gratings with the bread. Add two chopped green chillies, coriander leaves, half of the lemon juice, chilli powder and salt. Grind the mint leaves, and two green chillies into a paste and add the salt and the remaining lemon juice. Take half the potato mixture and roll out thick. Spread the mint

87

chutney over it. Roll out the remaining potato mixture and place over the mint chutney. Bake in the oven for 15 minutes at 300ºF. Cut into slices when cool, and serve hot.

Cabbage Rolls

4 large cabbage leaves
1 carrot, cubed
6 French beans, chopped
30 gms cottage cheese
½ cup mushrooms, chopped
½ tsp coriander powder
freshly ground black pepper to taste
1 tsp butter
salt to taste

Blanch the leaves in salted boiling water for 15 seconds. Blanch the carrots, beans and mushrooms also in salted boiling water for 3 minutes. Drain. Mix the cheese, vegetables, coriander powder, pepper and salt. Arrange two cabbage leaves, overlapping each other on one side of a flat ovenproof dish. Place half the vegetable-cheese mixture on the end of the leaves. Fold in the sides and roll, fixing a toothpick. Coat with half the butter. Do the same with the remaining cabbage leaves and other ingredients. Bake for 15 minutes and serve hot.

Stuffed Tomatoes

2 large tomotoes
75 gms moong dal, soaked

50 gms sultanas
2 spring onions, chopped
juice of ½ a lemon
freshly ground black pepper to taste

Slice the top off the tomatoes, and scoop out the flesh. Mix this pulp with the other ingredients, and then fill the tomatoes with this mixture. Serve garnished with some chopped coriander leaves or lettuce.

Stuffed Mushroom Omelette

50 gms mushrooms, grated
4 eggs, beaten till double in quantity
1 tsp oil
freshly ground black pepper to taste
a pinch of salt

Saute the mushrooms in oil in a non-stick pan. Pour the egg over the mushrooms till done. Remove from the fire and sprinkle the pepper on it. Cut into two and serve.

Upma

1 cup semolina, dry roasted
1 large onion, chopped
1 large carrot, diced
1 large capsicum, chopped
a handful of shelled peas
1 large piece of ginger, finely chopped
2 green chillies, chopped
curry and coriander leaves, chopped
1 tsp mustard
1 tsp Bengal gram
2 tbsps oil

salt to taste

Heat the oil, add the mustard seeds till they splutter and then add the Bengal gram and fry for a minute. Add the onions and fry till translucent. Add the chillies, ginger and curry leaves, fry for half a minute, then add the carrots, peas and capsicums. Fry for 2-3 minutes. Add 2¼ cups of water and salt. When the water starts boiling, add the semolina, lower the flame, and cover the pan for a minute. Then remove the lid and stir the mixture till the upma is dry. Garnish with the coriander leaves.

Wheat-Ragi Porridge

2 tbsps wheat, roasted

2 tbsps ragi, roasted

2 cups buttermilk

1 green chilli

1" small piece ginger

a small bunch of coriander leaves

½ tsp oil

1 tsp mustard

salt to taste

Powder the wheat and ragi. In one cup water, cook these till done. Grind together the chillies, ginger, coriander leaves and salt. Add this mixture to the buttermilk, and add the flour mixture. Mix well. Season with the mustard.

MAIN MEALS
Vegetable Pulao

150 gms basmati rice
220 gms shelled peas
2 large onions, chopped
1 large carrot, diced
1 small capsicum, chopped
½ cup chopped beans
1 clove garlic, finely chopped
1" piece ginger, finely chopped
1" piece cinnamon
2 cloves
2 green chillies, chopped
1 cardamom and bay leaf
1 bunch coriander leaves
a few mint leaves
2 tbsps oil
salt to taste

In hot oil, fry the cinnamon, cloves, bay leaf and cardamom for half a minute. Add the ginger, garlic and green chillies, and after a few seconds, add the onions. Fry for 5 minutes on low heat. Add the mint and coriander leaves and all the vegetables. Stir-fry for a couple of minutes. Then add the rice and salt and stir-fry for a minute. Add enough water so that it is half an inch above the mixture. Pressure cook till done. Garnish with the lemon wedges.

Pasta Amatriciana

150 gms pasta, cooked
100 gms bacon, chopped
1 onion, chopped

100 gms mushrooms, chopped
1 small capsicum, chopped
100 gms tomatoes, skinned and chopped
1 tsp tomato puree
1 clove garlic, chopped
125 ml water
¼ tsp chilli sauce
1 tsp chopped parsley
freshly ground black pepper
salt to taste

Cook the tomatoes, tomato puree, onion, garlic and bacon in water in a large saucepan over a medium heat for 10 minutes. Add the mushrooms, capsicum, chilli sauce, parsley, pepper and salt. Mix well, and cook for another 5 minutes, adding water if necessary. Arrange the pasta on a

plate and pour the bacon-sauce
mixture over the pasta. Serve hot.

Spinach-Peas with Rice

2 cups cooked rice

250 gms spinach

1 large onion, chopped

¼ cup shelled peas

1 tsp oil

1 tbsp tomato puree

1 cardamom, shelled

1 clove

½" piece ginger

2 flakes garlic

¼ tsp garam masala

¼ tsp chilli powder

salt to taste

a pinch of sugar

Pressure cook the spinach with onion, green chilli and 1 cup water. Remove, cool, and blend in a mixer. Heat oil in a non-stick pan, add the tomato puree. Crush the clove and cardamom and add to the puree. Crush the ginger and garlic and add to the puree. Stir well. Add the chilli powder, garam masala and salt, and after a few seconds of stir-frying, add the peas. Stir for a minute on low flame. Add the spinach puree and cover and cook on a medium flame till the mixture becomes thick.

Cauliflower with Garlic Sauce

1 small cauliflower, cut into florets
4 flakes garlic, crushed

1 green chilli, chopped
1 tbsp soya sauce
1 tsp tomato ketchup
½ tsp vinegar
coriander leaves, chopped
freshly ground pepper and salt to taste

Boil 1½ cups water with ¾ tsp salt. Add the cauliflower and boil for 2-3 minutes till soft. Strain. In hot oil fry the garlic and green chillies till the garlic changes colour. Remove from fire. Add the soya sauce, tomato sauce and vinegar. Return to heat and cook for a minute on very low flame. Add the coriander leaves and stir-fry for half a minute. Add two tablespoons of water and boil. Add the florets and pepper, and stir-fry for 5 minutes. Serve with hot chapaties.

Kabuli Chana with Potatoes

   1 large potato, boiled and cut into chunks

   ¼ cup boiled chanas

   2 tsps chopped coriander leaves

   1 tsp sugar

   ½ tsp chilli powder

   ½ tsp cumin seeds, roasted and powdered

   ½ tsp maida

   salt to taste

   juice of ½ a lemon

Mix together the sugar, salt, chilli powder, cumin powder and ¼ cup water in a pan and boil. Add the *maida*, dissolved in one tbsp water, stirring continuously. Boil for 3 minutes on low flame. Add the potatoes and *chana*, and cook till thick. Garnish with the coriander leaves, and serve hot with rice or chapaties.

Vegetable Sambhar

¼ cup red gram (arhar dal), cooked

½ cup cooked vegetables (peas, beans, carrots, pumpkin, drumsticks, onions, potatoes)

1 tsp mustard

1 tsp sambhar powder

a pinch of asafoetida

small lemon-sized ball of tamarind (juice extracted)

curry and coriander leaves, chopped

1 tsp ghee

salt to taste

Heat the ghee, add the mustard till the seeds splutter, add the asafoetida and curry leaves, then add the tamarind juice. Add the salt and all the vegetables. Add the sambhar powder and simmer for 5 minutes on medium heat. Add the gram, and cook for another 5 minutes. Remove from fire, and garnish with the coriander leaves. Serve hot with idlis or plain rice.

Baked Fish Almonds

125 gms fish steaks
1 onion, chopped
1 capsicum, chopped
2 tsps fish sauce

2 tsps lemon juice

1 tsp chopped parsley

1 tsp ground coriander seeds

1 tsp olive oil

75 ml water

50 gms almonds, split

freshly ground black pepper and salt to
  taste

Put the fish, onion and capsicum in an ovenproof dish. Combine all the other ingredients, except the almonds, pour over the fish, cover and bake in a preheated oven at 400°F for 20 minutes. Remove the lid and bake for 5 more minutes. Toast the almonds until golden brown, and garnish the fish with these.

Chicken in Curd

½ chicken, cut into pieces

1 cup curd

½ tsp gram flour, roasted

1 tsp chopped coriander leaves

a pinch of turmeric powder

¼ cup freshly grated coconut

2 green chillies

½ cup groundnuts, roasted and powdered coarsely

1 tsp sesame seeds, roasted and powdered coarsely

1 tsp ghee

½ tsp cumin seeds

salt to taste

Grind the coconut and chillies to a fine paste. Mix with all the other ingredients. Pressure cook along

with the chicken for 15 minutes.
Heat ghee and fry the cumin seeds.
Pour over the chicken-curd
mixture.

Prawn-filled Tomatoes

4 large tomatoes
200 gms prawns, shelled and deveined
2 tsps ginger-garlic-green chilli paste
2 tsps chopped coriander leaves
2 tsps grated cheese
2 tsps butter
salt to taste

Chop the top from the tomatoes,
scoop out the pulp and sprinkle the
inside walls with salt and invert
them for half an hour. Mix the pulp
with the prawns, ground paste,

coriander leaves and cheese. Heat the butter and fry the mixture for 5 minutes on medium heat. Stuff the tomatoes with the mixture and recap the tomatoes. Steam for 5 minutes. Serve hot with chapaties.

Meat Kababs

2 cups cooked rice
1 cup meat, cut into 1" cubes
1 small onion, chopped
2 green chillies, chopped
2 tbsps chopped coriander leaves
½ tsp pepper powder
1 tsp butter
salt to taste

Saute the onion in a non-stick pan with half teaspoon butter till it is translucent. Add the chillies, salt and pepper, and cook for a minute. Run in a blender to a paste. Add the meat cubes and fry till it turns brown. Add the coriander leaves to it. Coarsely run the cooked rice in a blender. Shape rice into flat rounds. Fill with meat and form into cutlets. Coat with the remaining butter, and grill under a medium heat till done.

Spicy Vegetables

1 large brinjal, chopped

¼ piece bottlegourd, chopped

1 onion, chopped

100 gms mushrooms, chopped

1 tbsp olive oil

2 tbsps lemon juice

1 tsp paprika

1 tsp ground cumin seeds

2 tsps ground coriander powder
chilli sauce
freshly ground pepper and
salt to taste

Heat the olive oil, add the onion and saute for 5 minutes. Add the ground spices and stir. Pour 220 ml of water in a pan, add the brinjal and bottlegourd. Simmer for 10 minutes. Add the mushrooms and cook till the liquid is thick enough to coat the vegetables. Add the lemon juice, chilli sauce, pepper and salt, and serve hot with rice or chapaties.

Bisibelebhat

½ cup cooked rice
100 gms red gram (arhar dal), cooked
  soft

¼ tsp turmeric powder

¼ tsp fenugreek powder

a pinch of asafoetida

½ tsp ghee

250 gms vegetables, chopped

½ tsp sambhar powder

½ tsp mustard powder

1 tsp bisibelebhat powder

½ tsp cumin seeds

lemon-sized ball of tamarind

salt to taste

Add all the vegetables to the gram, add turmeric, fenugreek powder, olive oil, sambhar and bisibelebhat powder. When the vegetables are half-cooked, add the rice and salt. Cook with enough water for the rice to get cooked. Fry the mustard and cumin seeds and add to the cooked rice. Add the tamarind water until the mixture is well blended and thick.

Tomato Rice

    1 cup fresh tomato juice
    2 tbsps ghee
    ¼ tsp mustard
    1 tsp Bengal gram
    1" piece ginger, grated
    curry and coriander leaves, chopped
    ¼ cup freshly grated coconut
    1 cup water
    ½ cup rice
    salt to taste
    1 tsp cumin seeds, roasted and powdered

In hot oil, add the mustard and Bengal gram. Then add the ginger, curry leaves and coconut. Add the water and boil it with salt. Then add the rice, and cook till it is nearly done. Add the tomato juice and stir well. Add the cumin powder, and cook on low heat till the rice is completely cooked. Garnish with the coriander leaves.

Raw Papaya Kofta

1 medium unripe papaya, grated
4 potatoes, grated
1 cup Bengal gram flour
½ tsp turmeric powder
salt to taste

Add the grated papaya and potatoes to the boiling water and

cook till half done. Remove, cool, and squeeze out the water. Add to this all the other ingredients. Mix well and shape small balls of the mixture like koftas. Grill under medium heat until done.

Green Gram Khichdi

½ cup green gram (split)

½ cup rice

½ cup diced vegetables

1 tsp black pepper, coarsely ground

½ tsp cinnamon powder

2 cloves

1 tsp ghee

Heat the ghee in a pan. Add the spices, and fry for a few seconds. Add the rice and gram and stir-fry for 5 minutes on a low fire. Add two cups of boiling water and salt to taste, and cook on low flame till done.

Sago Khichdi

2 cups sago

6 green chillies, chopped

8 curry leaves

½ cup groundnuts, coarsely ground

1 tsp cumin seeds

1 cup grated coconut

1 cup coriander leaves, chopped

2 tbsps ghee

2 potatoes, diced and cooked

Soak sago in water for half an hour. Drain. Heat ghee, add the cumin seeds, then curry leaves and chillies. Add groundnuts and fry till the nuts are brown. Add the sago and fry till golden brown. Add salt and the potatoes, and on low heat stir-fry till the sago is soft and done. Garnish with the coconut and coriander leaves.

Langar Dal

> 2 cups whole black gram, soaked in water for 6 hours
>
> 2 tsps cumin seeds
>
> 2 tsps turmeric powder
>
> 2 tsps garam masala powder
>
> 4 onions, chopped fine
>
> 2 tbsps ginger-garlic paste
>
> ½ cup ghee
>
> 4 green chillies, whole

Pressure cook all the ingredients together except ghee with five cups of water till the dal is cooked and soft. Pour the ghee over it, and serve hot with chapaties or hot plain rice.

Chinese Fried Rice

250 gms rice

4 eggs

1 stalk celery, chopped

1 capsicum, chopped

2 spring onions, cut into rings with the stem

1 carrot, grated

¼ tsp pepper

a pinch of ajinomoto

1 tsp soya sauce

chilli sauce

2 tbsps oil

salt to taste

⅔ cups water

Beat the eggs well with salt and pepper. Pressure cook the rice with $1^2/_3$ cups water till nearly done. Pressure cook. In hot oil, scramble the eggs. Add the rice and soya sauce, and fry till the rice is fully cooked. Sprinkle a little ajinomoto over the rice, and add the vegetables. Garnish with the chilli sauce and green chillies in vinegar. If you are a non-vegetarian, you can add cooked chicken and prawns to the rice, stir-fry well before adding the vegetables.

Dal with Vegetables

100 gms lentils (masoor dal)
50 gms carrots, cut into 1" pieces

50 gms French beans, cut into 1" pieces

50 gms white pumpkin, cut into 1" pieces

50 gms potatoes, cut into 1" pieces

½ tsp turmeric powder

¼ tsp chilli powder

¼ tsp mustard seeds

2 red chillies

½" piece ginger, cut fine

8 tbsps oil

salt to taste

Cook the lentils with the curry leaves in $2\frac{1}{3}$ cups of water in a pressure cooker without covering with the lid. Add the vegetables, ginger, turmeric, chillies and salt. Pressure cook for 2 minutes. Season with the mustard and red chillies.

Prawn-Cauliflower Pasta

250 gms pasta, cooked and drained
250 gms prawns, peeled and deveined
250 gms cauliflower florets
2 tbsps oil
2 cloves garlic, chopped
1 tsp cumin seeds
1 tsp mustard
½ capsicum, finely chopped
1 tsp salad oil
salt to taste

Heat the oil and add the mustard and cumin till the seeds splutter. Add the garlic and fry till light brown. Add the florets and stir-fry for a minute or two till they turn golden. Lower the heat and cook for 5 minutes, stirring occasionally. Add

118

the capsicum, prawns and salt. Stir well. Cook for another 2-3 minutes. Before serving, add the drained pasta, sprinkle the salad oil, and toss together.

Cauliflower Paratha

250 gms wheat flour
125 gms finely grated cauliflower
½ tsp garam masala
1 tsp salt
½" piece ginger, grated
½ tsp chilli powder
2 tsps oil

Knead the flour with a little salt and water. Keep aside for half an hour. Mix all the other ingredients. Roll out small balls of dough, place the mixture in the centre, gather the

119

edges and pinch them together to cover the filling, forming balls. Roll out the parathas and fry in a non-stick pan with a little oil.

Stuffed Lady's fingers

500 gms small lady's fingers
1 large tomato, finely chopped
4 flakes garlic
2 tsp coriander powder
½ tsp chilli powder
½ tsp cumin seeds
½ tsp aniseeds (saunf)
2 tbsps oil
lemon juice
salt to taste

Remove the head and tip of each lady's finger, slit them slightly on one side. Grind the garlic and onion with the chilli and coriander powders. Fill each lady's finger with this paste. Heat the oil and fry the cumin and aniseed. Add the tomato and salt, and cook for 2-3 minutes. Now add the lady's fingers, cover and cook on slow fire till done. Sprinkle the lime juice over it, and serve hot with chapaties.

Lamb Tongue Curry

4 lamb tongues, cut into pieces
½ cup curd
2 tsps poppy seeds
2 tsps grated coconut
2 tsps coriander seeds
2 tsps sesame seeds
2 tsps garlic-ginger paste

4-5 almonds
1 onion, chopped
1 carrot, chopped
1 capsicum, chopped
salt and chilli powder to taste

Roast the poppy seeds, coriander and sesame seeds, almonds and coconut. Grind with 2 tablespoons of water to a fine paste. Mix the curd, ginger-garlic paste, salt and chilli powder. Coat the tongue pieces with this paste and leave to marinate. Heat the oil and fry the onions till brown. Add the vegetables and fry for 2-3 minutes. Add the tongue pieces with the masala, and 1 cup of water. Cover and cook for 15-20 minutes till tender.

Spicy Vegetable Pie

½ cup chopped beans

½ cup chopped carrots

½ cup cauliflower florets

1 large capsicum, chopped

½ cup grated cheese

½ cup breadcrumbs

½ cup peas

1 tsp ginger paste

2 tsps coriander-cumin powder

3 tbsps oil

freshly ground black pepper and salt to taste

Heat the oil and fry the ginger for a few seconds. Add all the vegetables, except the capsicum. Add the salt, pepper, half the coriander leaves and the coriander-cumin powder. Add half a cup of water, cover and cook for 10 minutes, then cool. In a baking dish, arrange a layer of vegetable, then sprinkle some cheese over the layer. Repeat this till all the vegetables and cheese are used up. Decorate the top with the capsicum and cheese. Bake for 30 minutes at 350^0F. Remove the lid, sprinkle the breadcrumbs on the pie, close the lid, and allow the pie to stay in the oven for 10 minutes. Remove from the oven and garnish with the coriander leaves.

Macaroni Mushroom Bake

3 cups macaroni
1 cup mushrooms, chopped
2 cups milk
2 tbsps plain flour
2 tbsps margarine
½ onion, chopped
½ cup grated cheese
pepper and salt to taste

Saute the onions, using half the margarine. Prepare the white sauce with the flour, milk and margarine. Add the salt and pepper, onion, cheese, mushrooms and macaroni. Mix well, and bake in a greased dish at 350ºF for 30 minutes.

Groundnuts-Potato-Spinach Treat

2 large potatoes, cubed and boiled
½ kg spinach
⅓ cup shelled groundnuts, boiled
1 onion, chopped
1 green chilli, chopped
2 tbsps tomato puree
1 clove, powdered
2 cardamoms, powdered
1" piece ginger, finely chopped
3-4 flakes garlic, finely chopped
½ tsp garam masala
½ tsp red chilli powder
½ tsp salt
a pinch of sugar

Pressure cook the onion, green chilli and spinach in 1 cup water till the first whistle. Then lower the flame, and heat for 5 minutes. Remove and cool. Blend in a mixer. Heat the oil and fry the tomato puree on low heat. Add the clove, cardamom, ginger and garlic, salt, chilli powder and garam masala. Stir-fry for a minute. Add the groundnuts and potatoes, after a minute add the spinach and sugar. Cover and cook on medium flame for 8-10 minutes. Serve hot with chapaties or rice.

Capsicum-Potato Masala

150 gms small capsicums, slit into fingers

1 large potato, slit into fingers

3-4 flakes garlic, crushed coarsely

3 tbsps tomato puree

1 tsp kasoori methi

1½ tsps coriander powder
½ tsp garam masala
½ tsp chilli powder
¼ tsp sugar
2 tsps oil
salt to taste

Heat the oil and fry the garlic for ½ a minute. Add the tomato puree, kasoori methi, coriander powder, garam masala, chilli powder and sugar. Stir-fry, after mixing well, for a minute. Add the potato slits, and on medium flame, cook for 2 minutes. Add the capsicums and ¼ cup water. Stir-fry for 5 minutes. Serve hot with chapaties.

Mooli Paratha

1 cup wheat flour
125 gms radish, grated
25 gms ghee
½ tsp chilli powder
½ tsp garam masala
¼ cup coriander leaves
1 tsp pomegranate seeds
¼ tsp ajwain (thymol seeds)
½ tsp chopped chillies
salt to taste

Mix the flour and salt, and knead into a dough with water. Add salt to the radish, mix well, and squeeze out the water. Wash well, and again squeeze out the water. Add all the ingredients, except the ghee to it.

Mix well. Roll out the dough balls, fill with the stuffing, close and roll out again. Roast on a hot tava, adding 1 teaspoon ghee on each side. Serve hot with pickles and yoghurt.

Cheese-Vegetable Curry

1 cup cheese, cubed

2 cups mixed chopped vegetables (carrot, cauliflower, potato and capsicum)

2 big onions, chopped

1 cup milk

¼ cup tomato sauce

1 tsp ginger-garlic paste

1 tbsp flour (maida)

2 tbsps oil

1 tsp chilli powder

½ tsp cumin powder

½ tsp chat masala

1 tsp salt

Heat 1 teaspoon hot oil and saute the flour in it for a few seconds. Add the milk and stir till thick. Remove from the fire, and add the sauce. Stir well. In the remaining oil, fry the onion and pastes for 2 minutes. Add the vegetables, cheese, and the remaining ingredients. Cook till the consistency is thick.

Mango Rice

¾ cup rice, cooked

1 large mango, grated

2 red chillies

2 tsps coriander seeds

1 tsp cumin seeds

½" piece cinnamon
1 tsp Bengal gram
1 tsp black gram
½ tsp mustard
¼ cup groundnuts, roasted
1 sprig curry leaves
a pinch of asafoetida
½ tsp fenugreek
¼ tsp turmeric powder
2 green chillies
salt to taste

Roast together and powder the red chillies, coriander, cumin, fenugreek, cinnamon, cloves, Bengal and black grams and asafoetida. Heat the oil, and add the mustard till the seeds splutter. Add the mango, salt, turmeric and curry

leaves. Cook till the mango gratings
are done. Remove from fire. Add the
roasted powder. Mix with rice, and
garnish with groundnuts.

Methi Roti

1 cup flour
½ cup besan flour
1 bunch methi leaves, chopped
¼ bunch coriander leaves, chopped
½ tsp turmeric powder
2 tbsps oil or ghee
salt to taste

Mix together both the flours. Add
the salt, both kinds of the leaves, and
1 tsp ghee. Knead with very little
water into a soft dough. Roll out
small balls of dough and fry on a

non-stick pan with a little oil. Serve hot.

Lettuce-Dal Curry

a bunch of lettuce leaves, chopped and boiled

½ cup red gram, cooked

2 tbsps coconut gratings

2 red chillies

1 onion, chopped

¼ tsp turmeric powder

½ lemon

2 tsps oil

salt to taste

Mix together the lettuce and red gram. Grind the coconut with the chillies and turmeric. Add to the lettuce-dal mixture. Fry the onion till translucent. Add the mixture and

134

salt, and boil together for 3-4 minutes. Serve hot with rice or chapaties.

Some Useful Tips

- Brown bread is better than white bread.
- Use a non-stick pan and a griddle.
- Develop a liking for tea without sugar — it maybe difficult at first, but gradually you will get used to it, and will help you shed excess weight.
- One or two Marie biscuits can be taken with tea to ward off hunger.
- Avoid using processed or tinned foods.
- You can use cottage cheese but only once a week.

135

- Avoid the use of salt in salads — instead use freshly ground pepper and lemon juice.
- In recipes that are bland, use herbs and spices to flavour your food — thymol, mint, coriander leaves, fenugreek, asafoetida.
- Green chutney — mint and coriander — can be prepared and stocked in fridge, and used to make the low fat meals tastier.
- To reduce appetite, reach out for a glass of water, and drink it slowly — a good substitute for all those in-between meals snacks!
- If you are bored with eating salads day in and day out, you can use the vegetables without oil in chapaties

(mixed with the flour dough) and curd.

- Fresh salad of fruits, vegetables or sprouts is a healthy accompaniment to chapaties with different vegetable stuffings.
- Caloriewise, 1 cup of boiled rice is equivalent to 2 small chapaties.
- Use vegetables with high fibre and water content — radish, carrot, cucumber, cabbage, tomato — for salads.
- Use more raw tomatoes than onions as one tomato has only one-third the calories of an onion.
- Tomatoes are higher in calorie content than radish, cabbage and cucumber.

- If you are still hungry after your meal, take more salads or 1 more chapati instead of a helping of cooked vegetables.
- Less oil is good for the whole family.
- Ensure that your major portion of food consists of cereals which takes a longer time to digest, keeping you satisfied longer.
- Remember that red chillies are said to increase your after-meal metabolic rate, thus burning more calories.
- Add spinach or bottlegourd (*ghia*) to dal for more nutritive value and fibre content.
- If you go to parties, and enjoy eating a good meal, always remember to

eat a very light meal the next day —
a light soup, or only plenty of fruits,
or salads with a little curd.

Calorie Guidance

Vegetables	*Cals.*
Brinjal, 100 gms	24
Beetroot, cooked, ½ cup	34
Cabbage, chopped, ½ cup	12
Carrot, large, 1	42
Cauliflower, cooked, ½ cup	15
Chillies green, 100 gms	29
Coriander leaves, 100 gms	48
Corn, boiled, 1	84
Cucumber, medium, ½	6
Drumstick, 100 gms	26
French beans, 100 gms	26
Lady's fingers, 8	28
Lettuce, 3 leaves	5
Mint, 100 gms	48
Onion, average, 1	45
Peas, cooked, ½ cup	56
Potato, boiled, medium, 1	83
Pumpkin, cooked, ½ cup	33

	Cals.
Radish, 100 gms	17
Spinach, cooked, ½ cup	23
Tomato, medium, 1	20
Yam, 100 gms	111

Fruits	*Cals.*
Apple, medium, 1	66
Banana, medium, 1	132
Figs, small, 3	79
Grapefruit, medium, ½	72
Grapes, 22-24	70
Guava, medium, 1	42
Mango, 1	122
Melon, medium, ½	37
Orange, medium 1	68
Papaya, medium, ⅓	50
Peach, medium, 1	32
Pear, 1	84
Pineapple, 1 slice	44
Plum, 1	30
Pomegranate, 100 gms	90
Sweet lime, average, 1	63
Watermelon cubes, 100 gms	28

Cereals and Cereal Foods	*Cals.*
Bajra flour (30 gms) chapati, 1	108
Barley, 2 tbsps	99

Jawar flour 30 gms		
chapati, 1		106
Macaroni, cooked, 2/3 cup		107
Maize flour 30 gms		
chapati, 1		102
Oatmeal porridge, 1 cup		148
Rice, boiled, 1 cup		138
Wheat bread, 1 slice		75
Wheat flour (30 gms)		
chapati 1		70
Wheat paratha, 60 gms		
with 2 tsps fat,		256

Pulses		*Cals.*
Bengal gram, roasted,	100 gms	369
Bengal gram	200 gms,	
Black gram	1 cup	
Green gram	cooked	105
Lentil	thin	
Red gram	dal	

Milk and Milk Products	*Cals.*
Buttermilk, 1 cup	62
Cheese, cheddar, 28 gms	111
Cheese, cottage, 1 tbsp	27
Cream, 2 tbsps	56
Curd (buffalo milk), 1 cup	182

Ice-cream, 100 gms	96
Milk (buffalo's), 1 cup	206
Milk (buffalo's), skimmed, 1 cup	78
Milk (cow's), 1 cup	160
Milk (cow's), skimmed, 1 cup	70
Milk, condensed, 1 tbsp	62

Dried Fruits and Nuts	*Cals.*
Currants, ½ cup	268
Figs, dried, 2	81
Raisins, 1 tbsp	27
Almonds, 12-15	90
Cashewnuts, 6-8	88
Coconut, 1 piece	54
Coconut water, 1 glass	46
Groundnuts, roasted, 1 tbsp	86
Pistachio, 30	88
Walnuts, 8 halves	128

Fats and Oils	*Cals.*
Butter, 1 tsp	36
Ghee, 1 tsp	45
Oil (groundnut), 1 tbsp	160
Oil (sesame or til), 1 tbsp	126

Beverages	*Cals.*
Cocoa, 1 tbsp with cow's milk, 1 cup	224
Coffee, 1 cup with 2 tbsp cow's milk and 2 tsp sugar	60
Tea, 1 cup with 2 tbsp cow's milk and 2 tsp sugar	60
Sweet Items	*Cals.*
Chocolate, nut, 1 piece	142
Glucose, 1 tbsp	45
Honey, 1 tbsp	64
Jaggery, 1 tbsp	56
Sugar, 1 tsp	20
Sugar, 1 cube	24
Cake, sponge, 50 gms	153
Custard, 150 gms	205
Jelly, 65 gms	65
Miscellaneous	*Cals.*
Egg, hen's, 100 gms	173
Fish, 100 gms	195
Egg, duck's, 100 gms	181
Beef, 100 gms	114
Pork, 100 gms	114
Mutton, 100 gms	194

Health Without Harm

- Walking is the beacon of light in the fitness gloom.
- None of the injuries common to other sports is seen in walking.
- Walking is inherently safe if ordinary care is taken.
- As a precautionary measure, increase the walking distance and speed gradually over several weeks.
- Always do some warm-ups before taking a long walk.
- Walking should be moderate in distance and intensity.
- After walking for an hour or more, cool down slowly.

- Blisters can be caused by repeated friction of the bottoms of the toes, by too much pressure from the front of the shoe — hence ensure that you wear proper shoes.
- Blisters can be prevented by applying a little petroleum jelly on the undersurfaces of the toes.
- An injury to a toenail can lead to bleeding in the nail bed, causing the nail to become black — hence clip the nails short and round them with an emery board.
- Heat is but one environmental agent that walkers have to watch — hence take a brisk walk the first thing in the morning when it is still cool.

- Allergic people should also take adequate protection against humidity, pollution, cold and pollen grains.
- Use a sunscreen lotion to block ultraviolet rays, but use it sparingly to allow free evaporation of perspiration.
- In extremely cold weather, it is better not to exercise too vigorously out in the open.
- If you are asthmatic, and use medication, take the medication before exercising in the cold.
- Just select the right outfit, keep a good measure of common sense about you, and then start walking.

- The initial shock of stepping out into the cold can be softened by an indoor warm-up.
- Preferably, do not walk near main roads as carbon monoxide emitted by vehicles can be injurious to your cardiovascular performance, thus cancelling out the major benefits of fitness training and performance ability.
- Remember that there is safety in numbers, which discourages pillage, rape or mugging.
- Another precautionary measure is to walk against traffic when possible.
- Fitness walking, a universal stress reliever, energises you, helps you to

relax, and to cope with anything that life throws at you, especially in the workplace.

- Fitness walking can help you to tackle and handle back pain, arthritis, varicose veins, hypertension, respiratory problems, heart diseases, cholesterol, premenstrual syndrome and cardiac rehabilitation.

- When you walk briskly, you burn off around 200 calories every 30 minutes, and your raised metabolic rate will continue to burn up calories for several hours after you have finished exercising.

- Walking regularly tightens the muscles of your hips, thighs and

148

buttocks, burning away unwanted fat, and helping you get back to a trim and attractive shape.

- Fitness walking, especially aerobic walking, is the easiest way to deal with tension, anxiety and stress.
- A pregnant woman should consult her doctor before commencing or continuing a fitness walking programme.
- A good walk daily during pregnancy can help you to prevent high blood pressure, fatigue, backache and discomforts that one experiences during this time.
- Postnatal walking is an excellent form of exercise.

- Anyone suffering from premenstrual syndrome, when headaches, backaches, depression and extreme tiredness are frequent, should find relief from regular walking.
- A regular walk promotes muscular development, and joint flexibility increases circulation, and relaxes the body.
- People who sit down for lengthy periods during the day need to get up and walk at regular intervals to avoid lower-back pain.
- If you have varicose veins, and are overweight, take things easy, and start a walking programme of 10

minutes to begin with, at a steady and slow pace.

- People having osteoporosis should follow a good calcium diet, and exercise by walking regularly.

- People who give up smoking complain that they tend to put on weight because they eat more snacks, but this is where fitness walking can be of great benefit by helping in weight control.

- A brisk walk in the fresh air also helps to take your mind off any craving you may have for a puff.

- Regular fitness walking, along with a low-fat, high-fibre diet, being an excellent form of weight control, can remarkably help in reducing high blood pressure.

- Avoid smoking, intake of alcohol and caffeine, and ensure a low-salt, low-sugar, low-fat diet to help reduce high-blood pressure.
- A regular, vigorous exercise like brisk walking can reduce the risk of a heart attack by half.
- People afflicted with arthritis suffer from pain and depression, leading to lethargy, and walking in this case becomes a natural antidepressant, promoting feelings of well-being.
- The quickest way to calm the mind, relax, and get back in touch with your spiritual self is to walk.

- The feet that we use for walking allow us to collect energy from the ground — the earth.
- Breath control is one way of learning to meditate, another way is to walk.
- Brisk walking helps to clear dangerous fats from the blood, and reduces the chances of clogged arteries.

Benefits of Walking

- Walking increases the flow of oxygen to all tissues and cells.
- It increases the high-density lipoproteins (good cholesterol) which protects the heart and blood vessels from fatty deposits.
- It protects and strengthens the heart muscles whereby it can pump more blood with fewer beats.
- It increases the ability to handle stress successfully, making you less prone to blood pressure and heart disease.
- It decreases the sugar fats (triglycerides), thus preventing their

being deposited on the lining of the arteries.

- It increases the efficient functioning of exercising muscles and blood circulation so that the muscles and blood can process oxygen more easily.

- It increases the number and size of blood vessels for better and more efficient blood circulation.

- Walking favours more imaginative brain work by loosening the thinking process, and replacing straight line thinking by lateral and branched thinking, i.e., delving deeper into the mind.

- Walking is more conducive to web-like patterns of thinking.

- Closely related to deep thinking is the sense of peace and calmness that comes with walking at a proper pace.
- A proper walking rhythm, coupled with the repeated contact with the earth, helps you to achieve this pace.
- Walking for fitness will lead to health by better nutrition as well as by exercise *per se*.
- By its very nature, walking is a safe sport, a moderate exercise that is easy on all the tissues of the bones, joints, muscles, tendons and ligaments.
- A commitment to daily walking leads to an enjoyment of life that

you may never have experienced before.

- Walking reduces tension, and provides a forum for relaxation and unwinding.
- It aids in problem solving, and helps you to become mentally alert.
- Walking is a positive way to handle anger, improve your disposition and point of view, and even your sex drive.
- It is a pleasant distraction from a humdrum life, and promotes a sense of general well-being.
- It adds life to your years, and helps to develop a positive body image.
- Walking is non-competitive.

- It unclogs your mind, makes you self-reliant, and improves your posture.
- Regular walking also sets the stage for meditation and spiritual progress.
- Walking also has financial benefits to offer — walk more whenever and wherever you can, thus saving on transport charges.
- Walking saves you money at the petrol pump, and in car repairs and maintenance.
- It cuts down on the need for prescribed drugs.
- It saves on medical bills and hospitalisation costs.
- It helps in saving money, as there is no need to join a formal exercise or weight control programme.

- Walking does not necessarily require special equipment.
- It increases work productivity.
- It aids in resiliency and recovery from injuries.
- Brisk walking aids in sounder sleep, and promotes physical and mental health.
- It decreases appetite, and aids in digestion and elimination.
- It increases respiratory efficiency and cardiac output.
- It decreases the possibilities of degenerative disease.
- It increases energy reserves, and replaces fat with muscles.
- It improves the skin tone, and is a good preventive medicine.

Other titles in the series

- Relaxation
- Yoga
- Healing Powers of Water
- Weight Reduction
- First Aid
- Fitness
- Acne
- Anxiety
- Headache
- Heart Attack